Proverbs in Color

by Lovink

"Every
word of God
is flawless;
he is a shield
to those who
take refuge
in him."

Proverbs 30:5

"As iron sharpens iron, so one person sharpens another."

Proverbs 27:17

"Those
who conceal
their sins do
not prosper,
but those who
confess and
renounce them
find mercy."

Proverbs 28:13

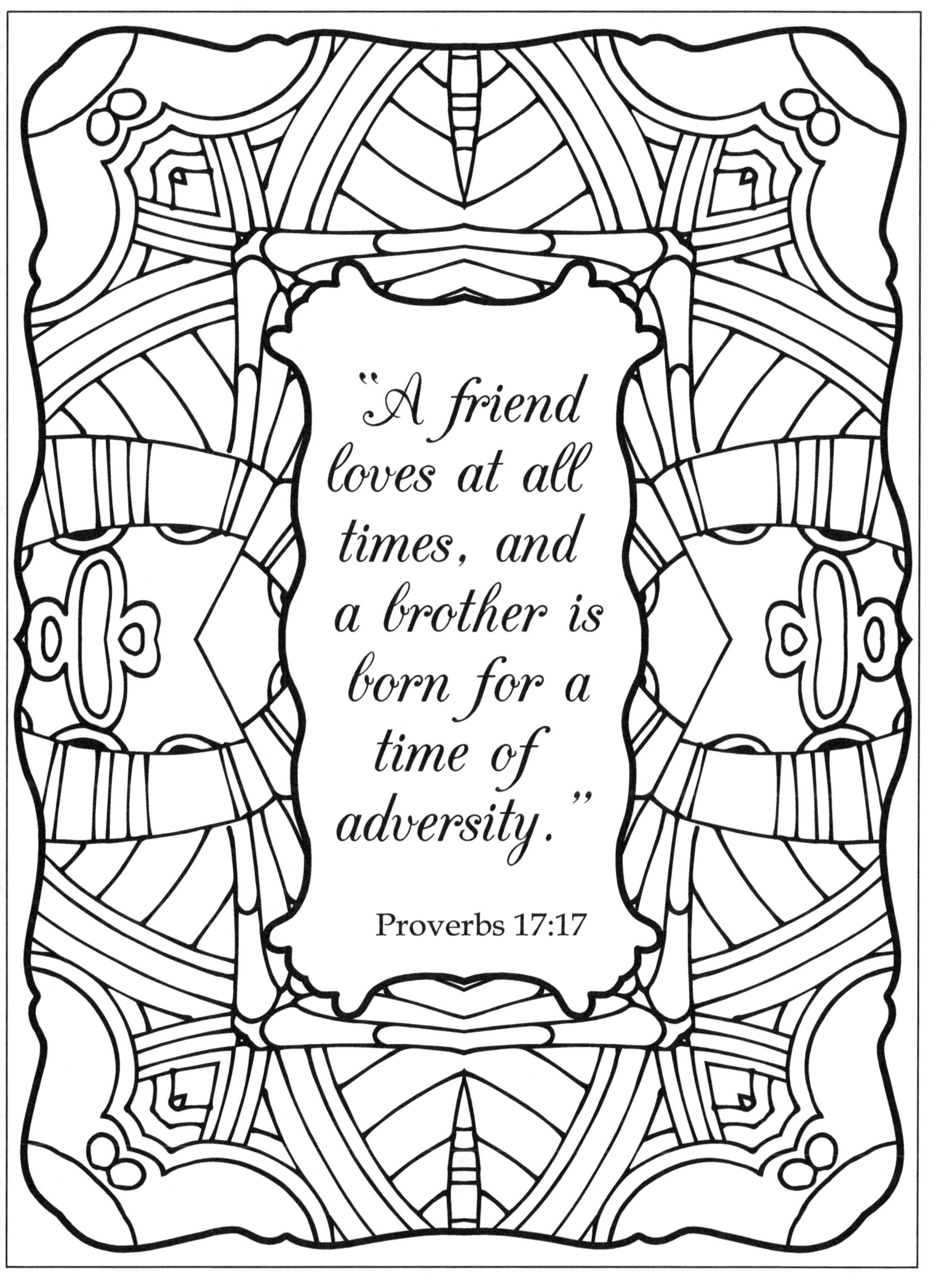

"A friend loves at all times, and a brother is born for a time of adversity."
Proverbs 17:17

"Get
wisdom, get
understanding;
do not forget my
words or turn
away from
them."

Proverbs 4:5

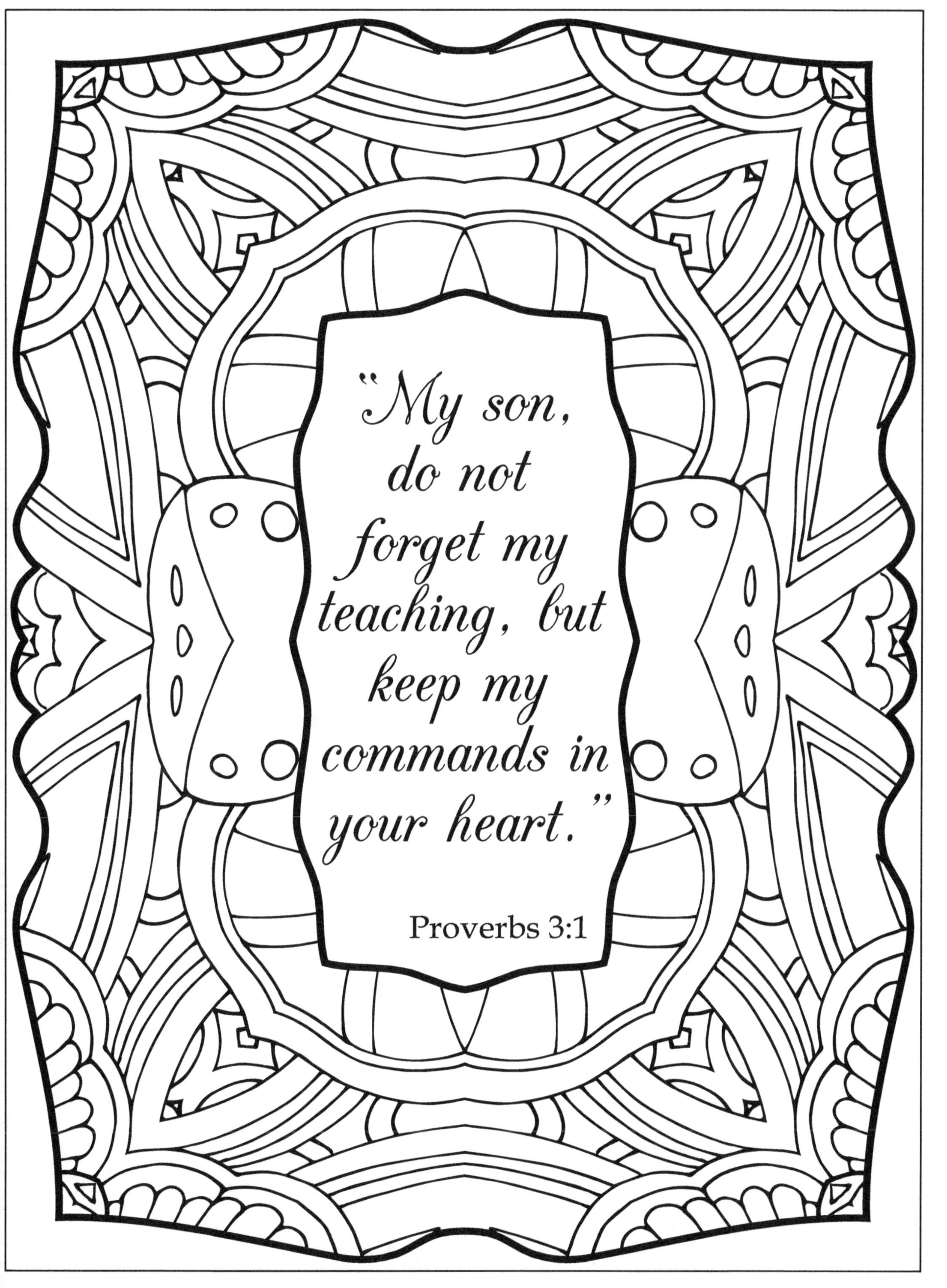

"My son, do not forget my teaching, but keep my commands in your heart."
Proverbs 3:1

"One who has unreliable friends soon comes to ruin, but there is a friend who sticks closer than a brother."

Proverbs 18:24

"Listen, my son, to your father's instruction and do not forsake your mother's teaching."

Proverbs 1:8

"Blessed are
those who
find wisdom,
those who
gain
understanding."

Proverbs 3:13

"Many are the
plans in a
human heart,
but it is the
Lord's
purpose that
prevails."

Proverbs 19:21

"A good
name is more
desirable than
great riches; to
be esteemed is
better than
silver or gold."

Proverbs 22:1

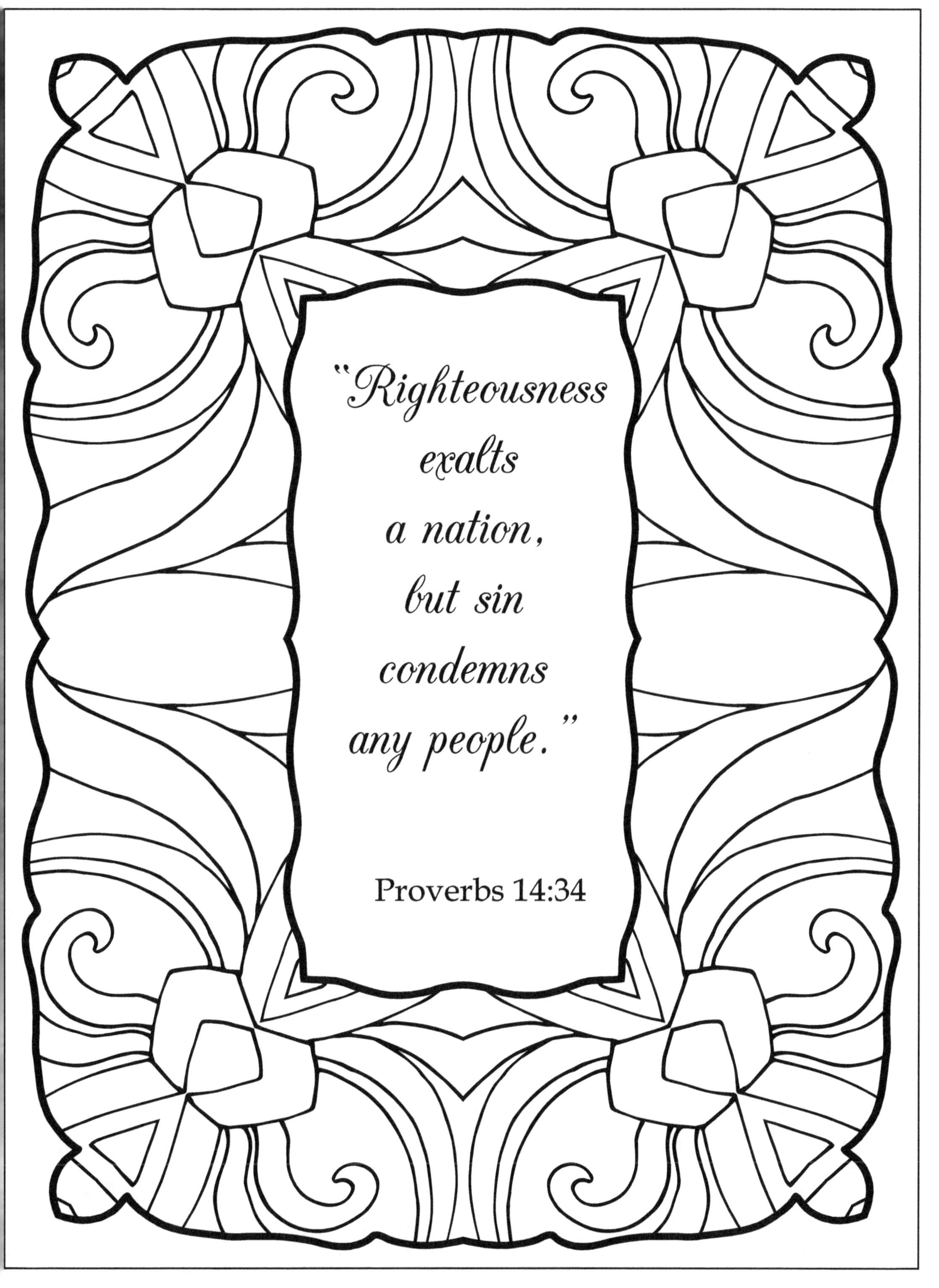

"Righteousness exalts a nation, but sin condemns any people."

Proverbs 14:34

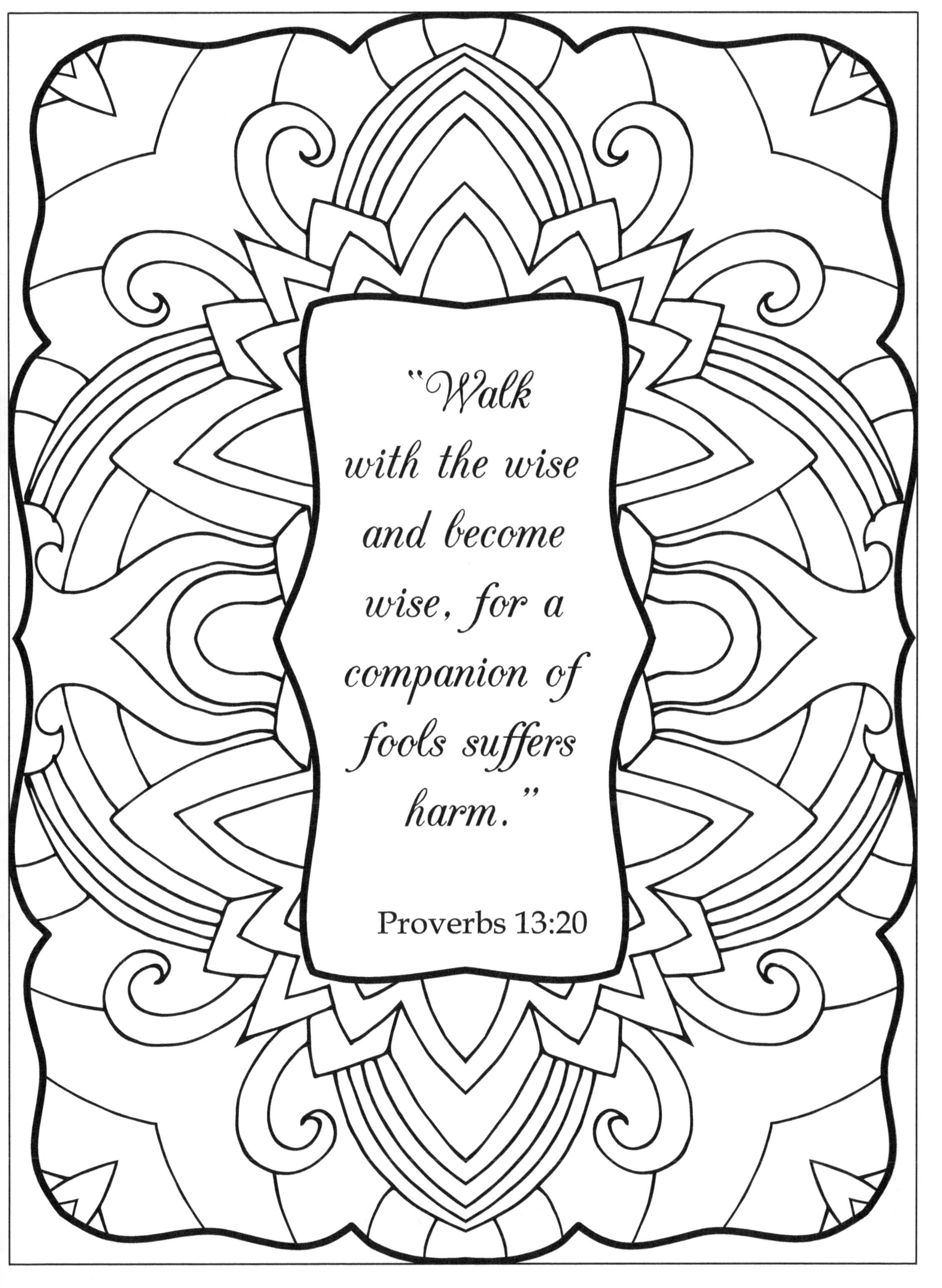
"Walk
with the wise
and become
wise, for a
companion of
fools suffers
harm."

Proverbs 13:20

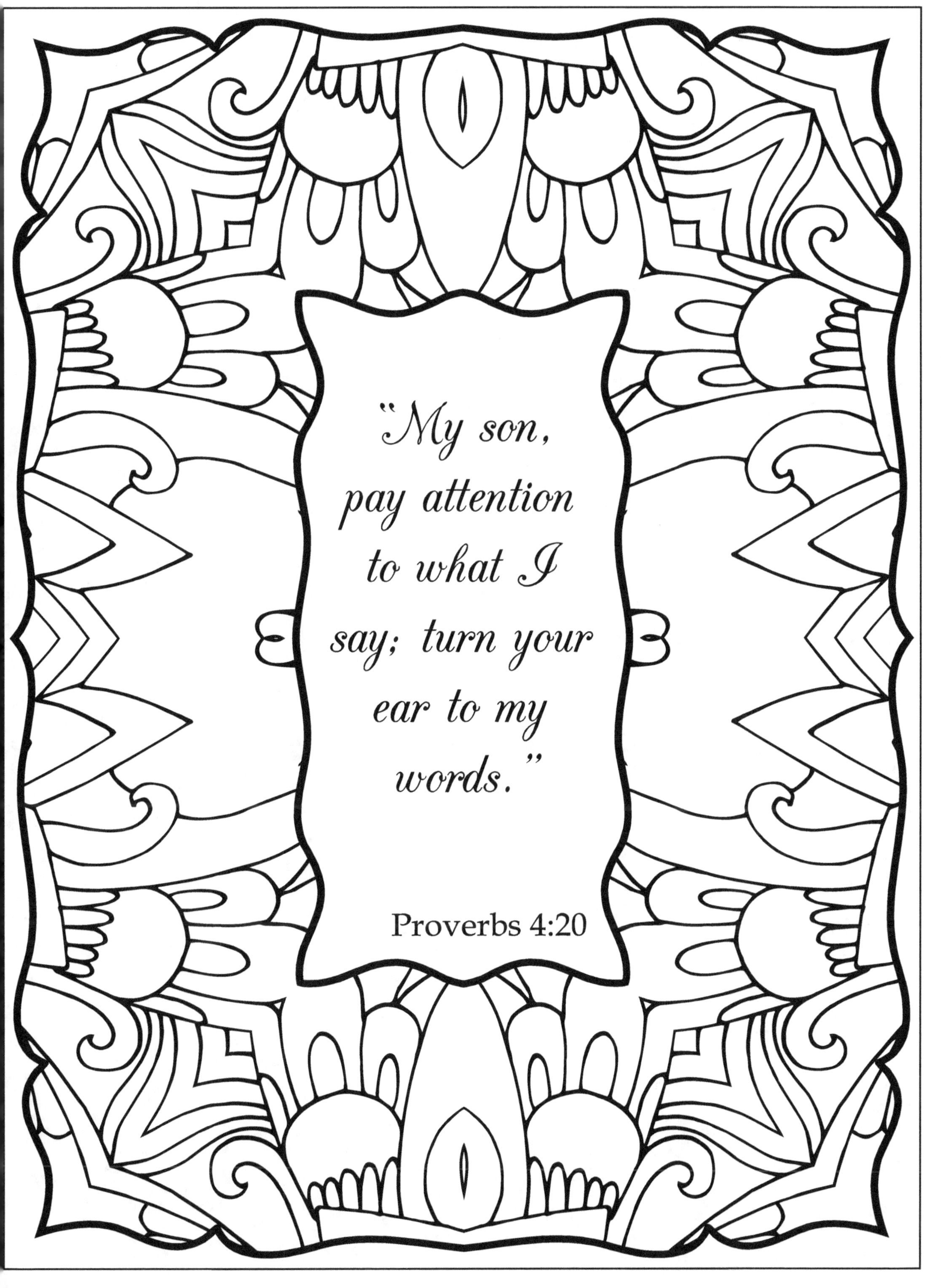
"My son,
pay attention
to what I
say; turn your
ear to my
words."

Proverbs 4:20

"The mouth of the righteous is a fountain of life, but the mouth of the wicked conceals violence."

Proverbs 10:11

"Speak up for those who cannot speak for themselves, for the rights of all who are destitute."

Proverbs 31:8

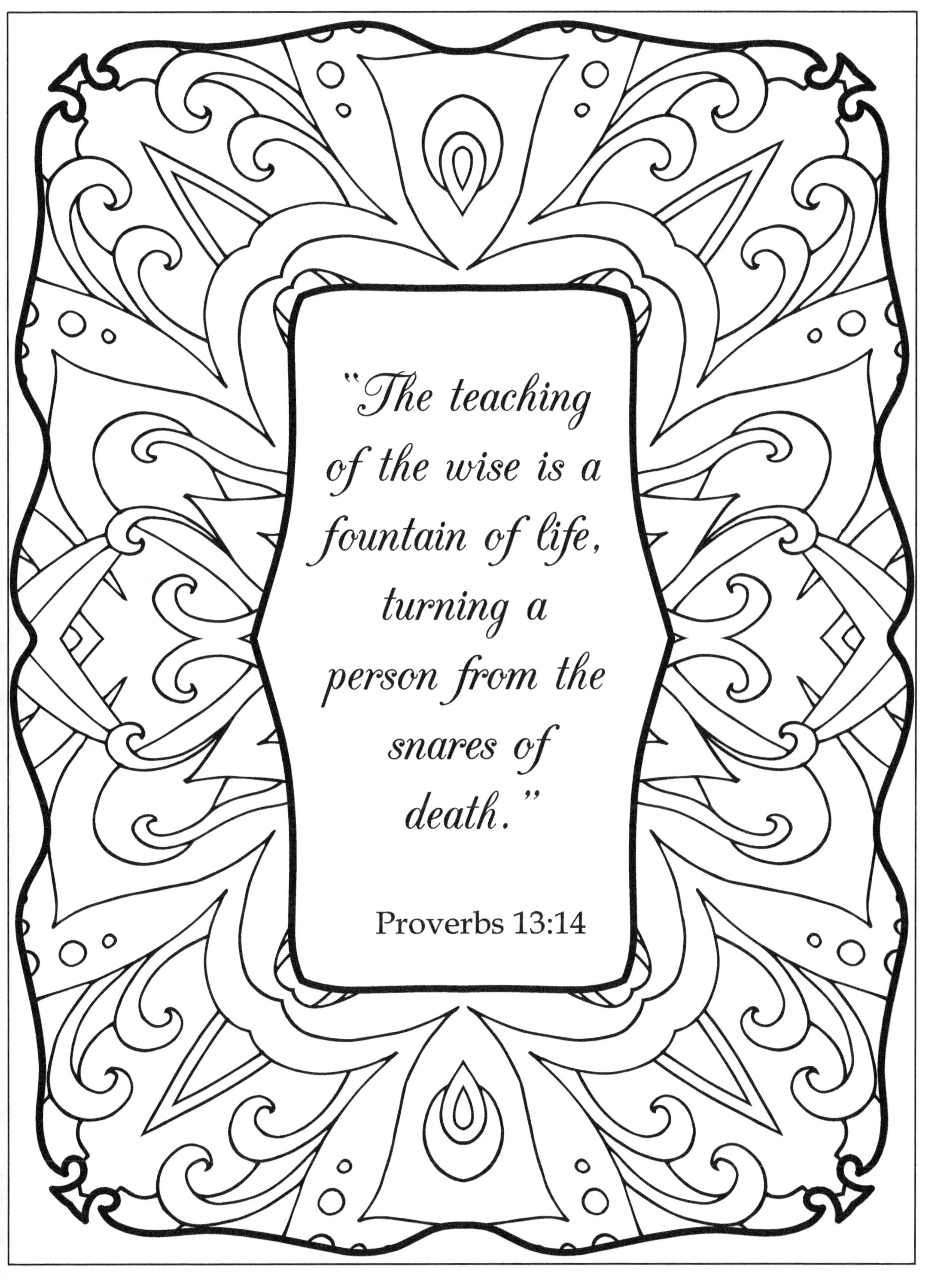
"The teaching
of the wise is a
fountain of life,
turning a
person from the
snares of
death."

Proverbs 13:14

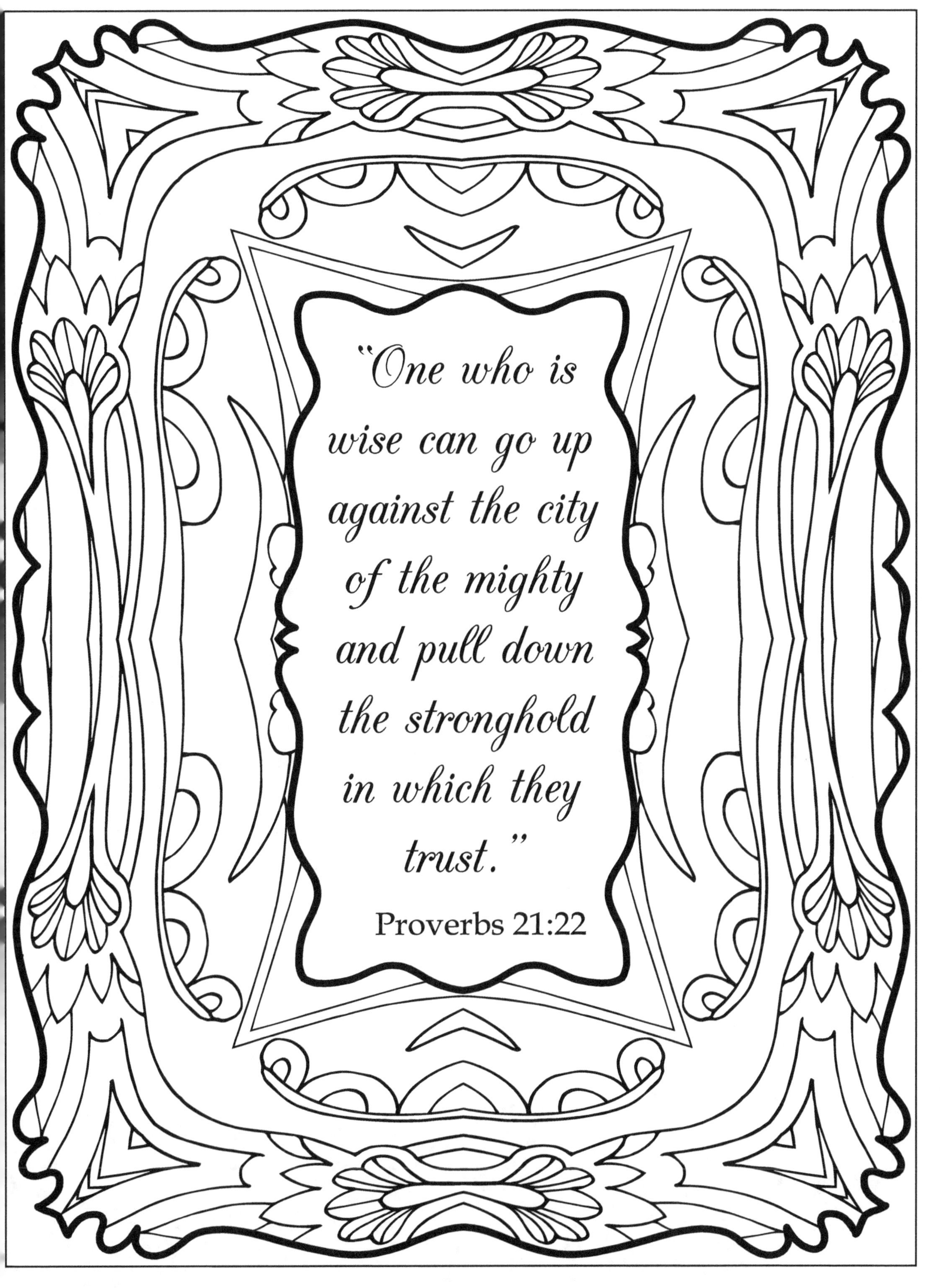

"One who is wise can go up against the city of the mighty and pull down the stronghold in which they trust."

Proverbs 21:22

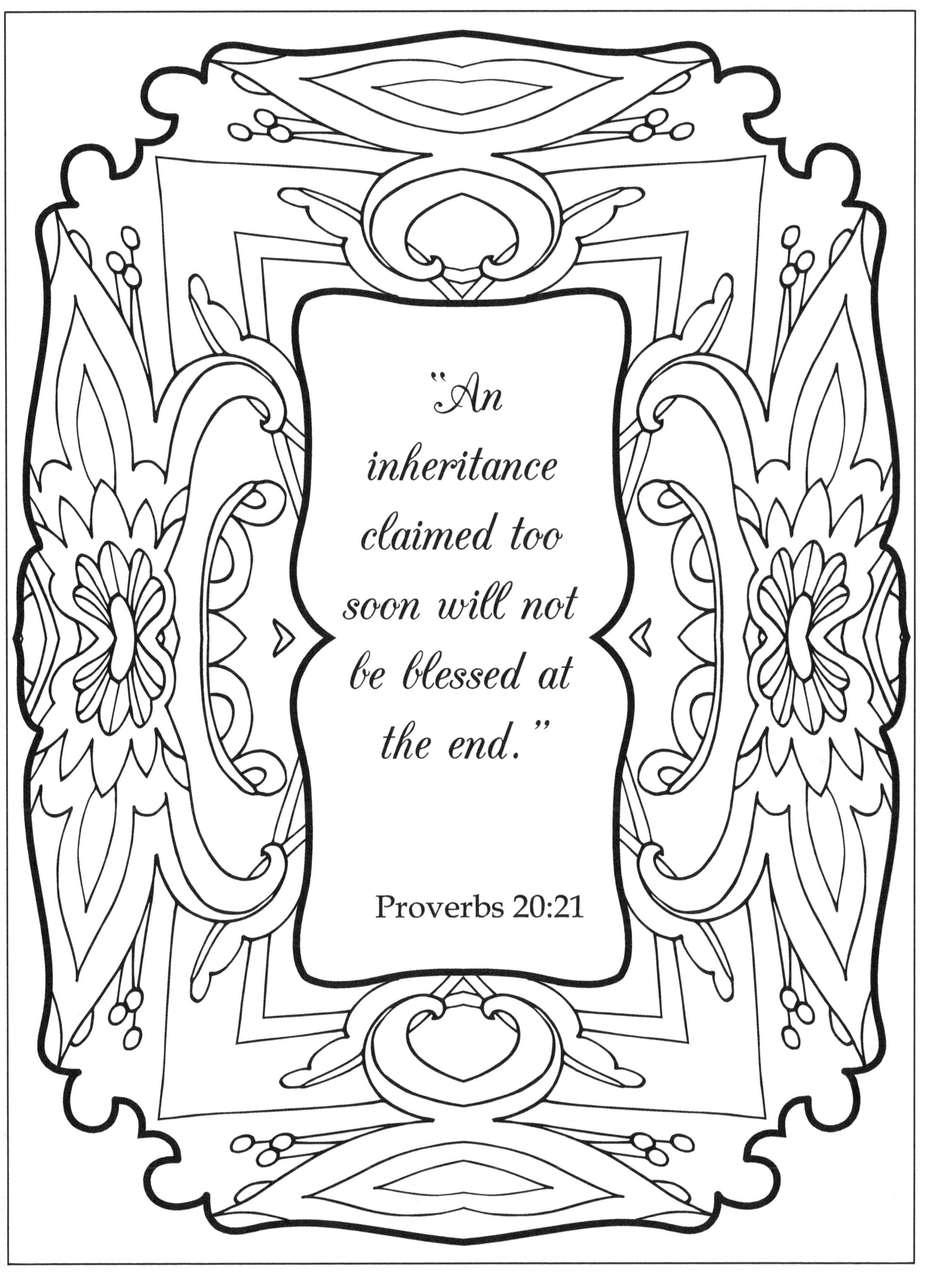

"An inheritance claimed too soon will not be blessed at the end."

Proverbs 20:21

"The path of
the righteous is
like the morning
sun, shining ever
brighter till the
full light
of day."

Proverbs 4:18

"Do not forsake wisdom, and she will protect you; love her, and she will watch over you."

Proverbs 4:6

"Choose my instruction instead of silver, knowledge rather than choice gold "
Proverbs 8:10

"The father
of a righteous
child has
great joy; a
man who
fathers a wise
son rejoices
in him."

Proverbs 23:24

"This will
bring health
to your body
and
nourishment
to your
bones."

Proverbs 3:8

"Better a
small serving
of vegetables
with love than
a fattened calf
with hatred."

Proverbs 15:17

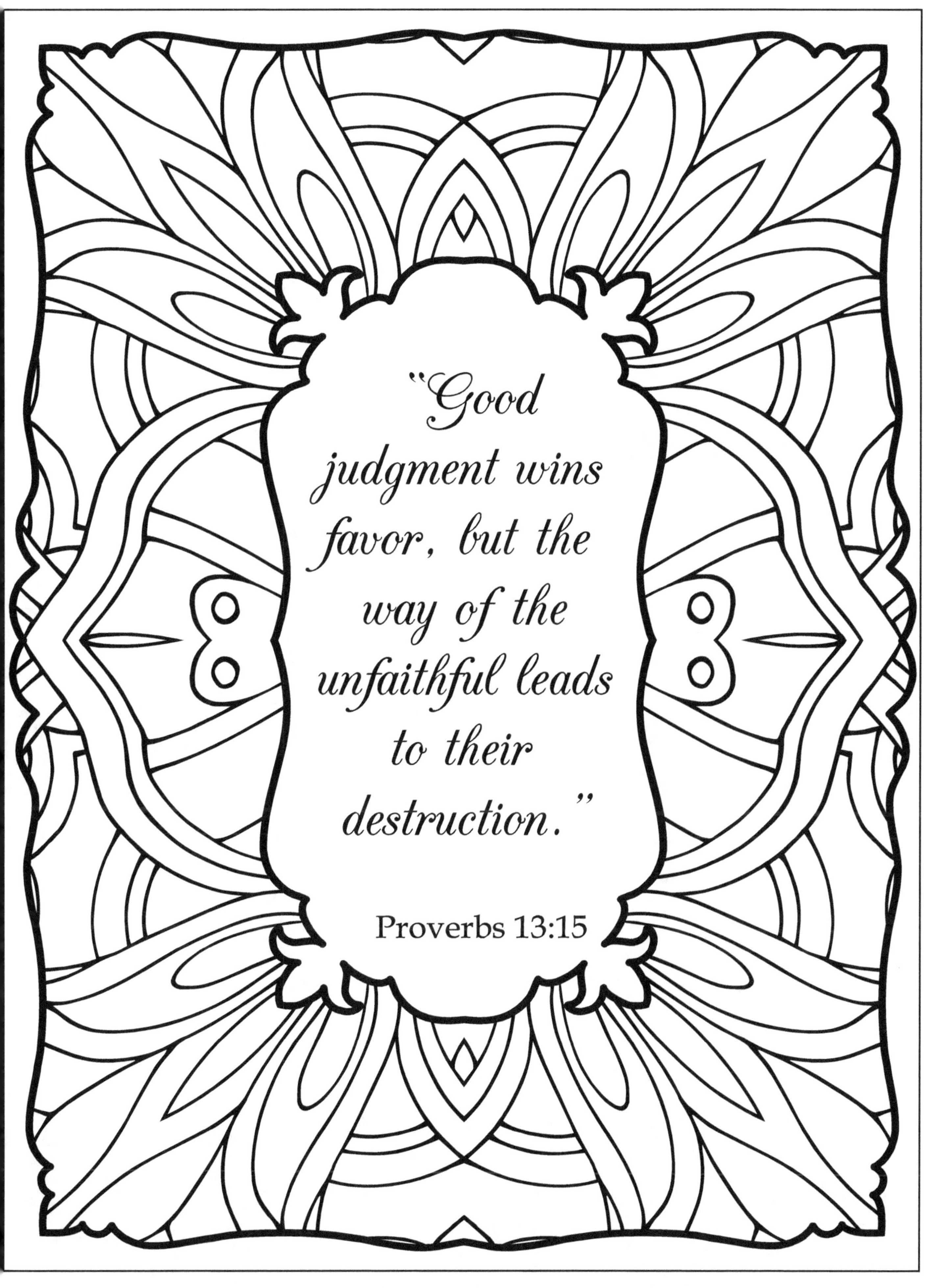
"Good judgment wins favor, but the way of the unfaithful leads to their destruction."

Proverbs 13:15

"For through wisdom your days will be many, and years will be added to your life."
Proverbs 9:11

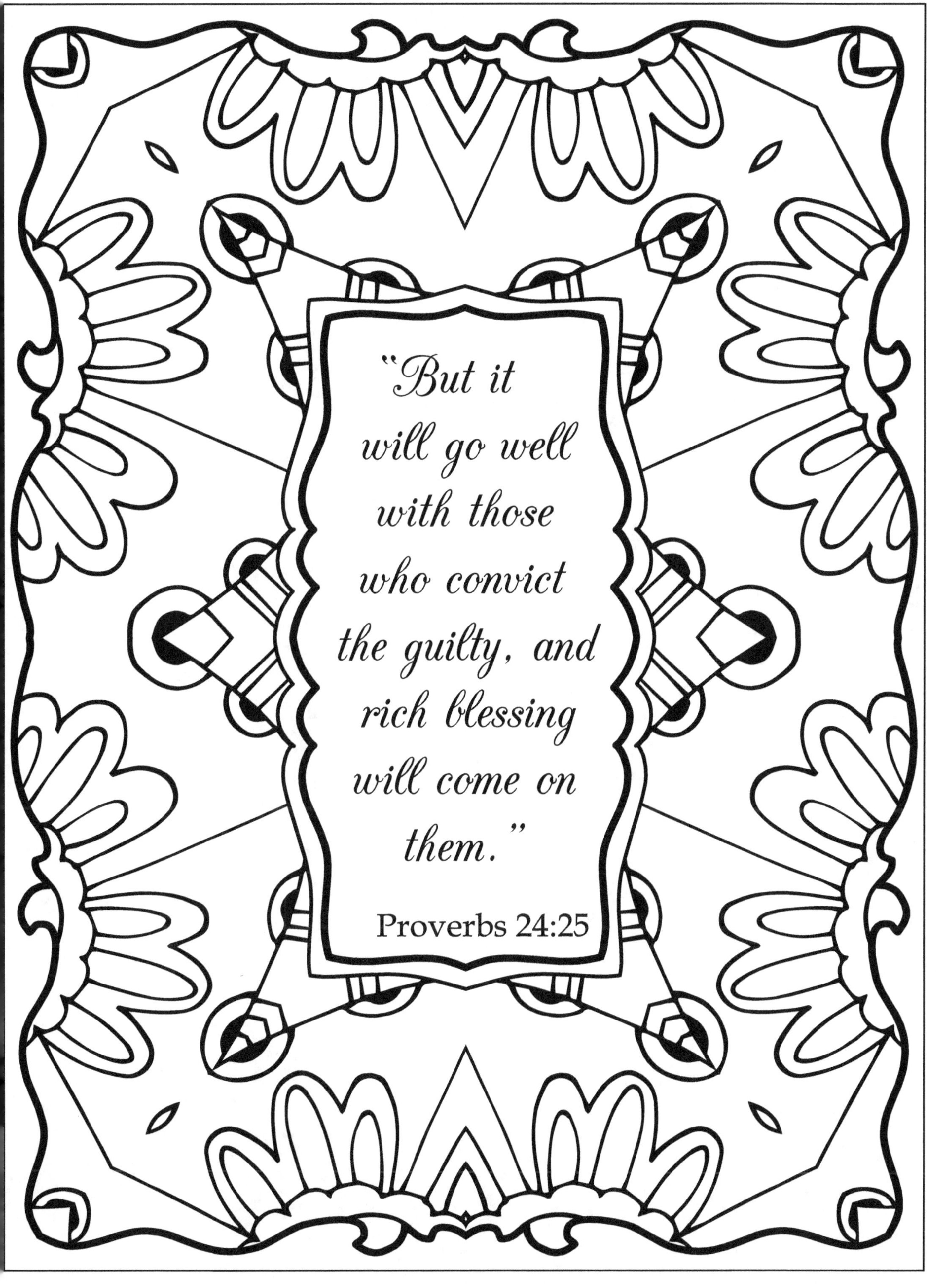
"But it
will go well
with those
who convict
the guilty, and
rich blessing
will come on
them."

Proverbs 24:25

"Now then, my sons, listen to me; do not turn aside from what I say."

Proverbs 5:7

"Cherish her, and she will exalt you; embrace her, and she will honor you."

Proverbs 4:8

Do not say,
"I'll pay you
back for
this wrong!"
Wait for the
Lord and he
will avenge
you.
Proverbs 20:22

"Better to be lowly in spirit along with the oppressed than to share plunder with the proud."

Proverbs 16:19

"Because the Lord disciplines those he loves, as a father the son he delights in."

Proverbs 3:12

"Then you will understand the fear of the Lord and find the knowledge of God."

Proverbs 2:5

"Those who
are kind
benefit
themselves,
but the cruel
bring ruin on
themselves."

Proverbs 11:17

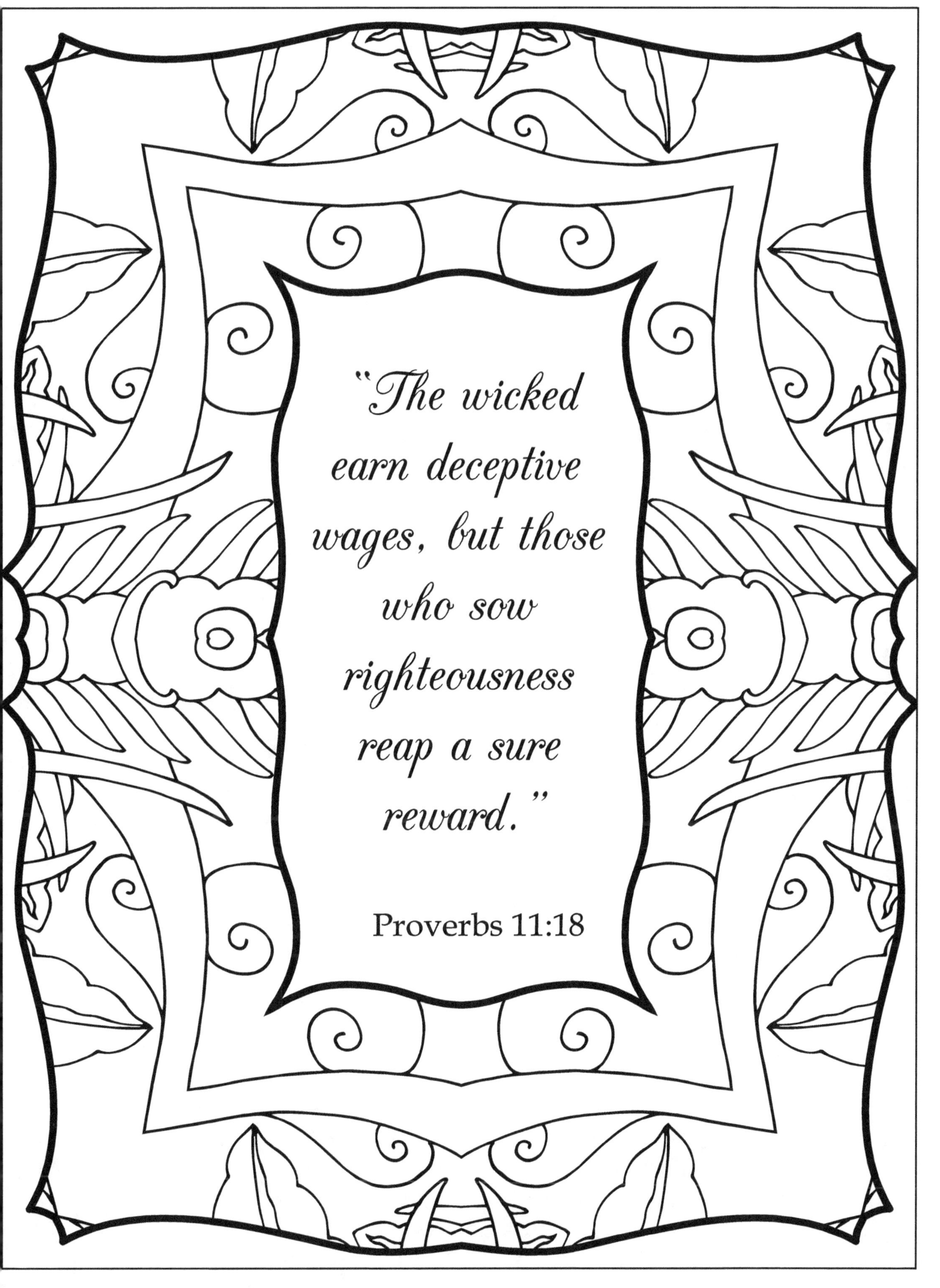

"The wicked earn deceptive wages, but those who sow righteousness reap a sure reward."

Proverbs 11:18

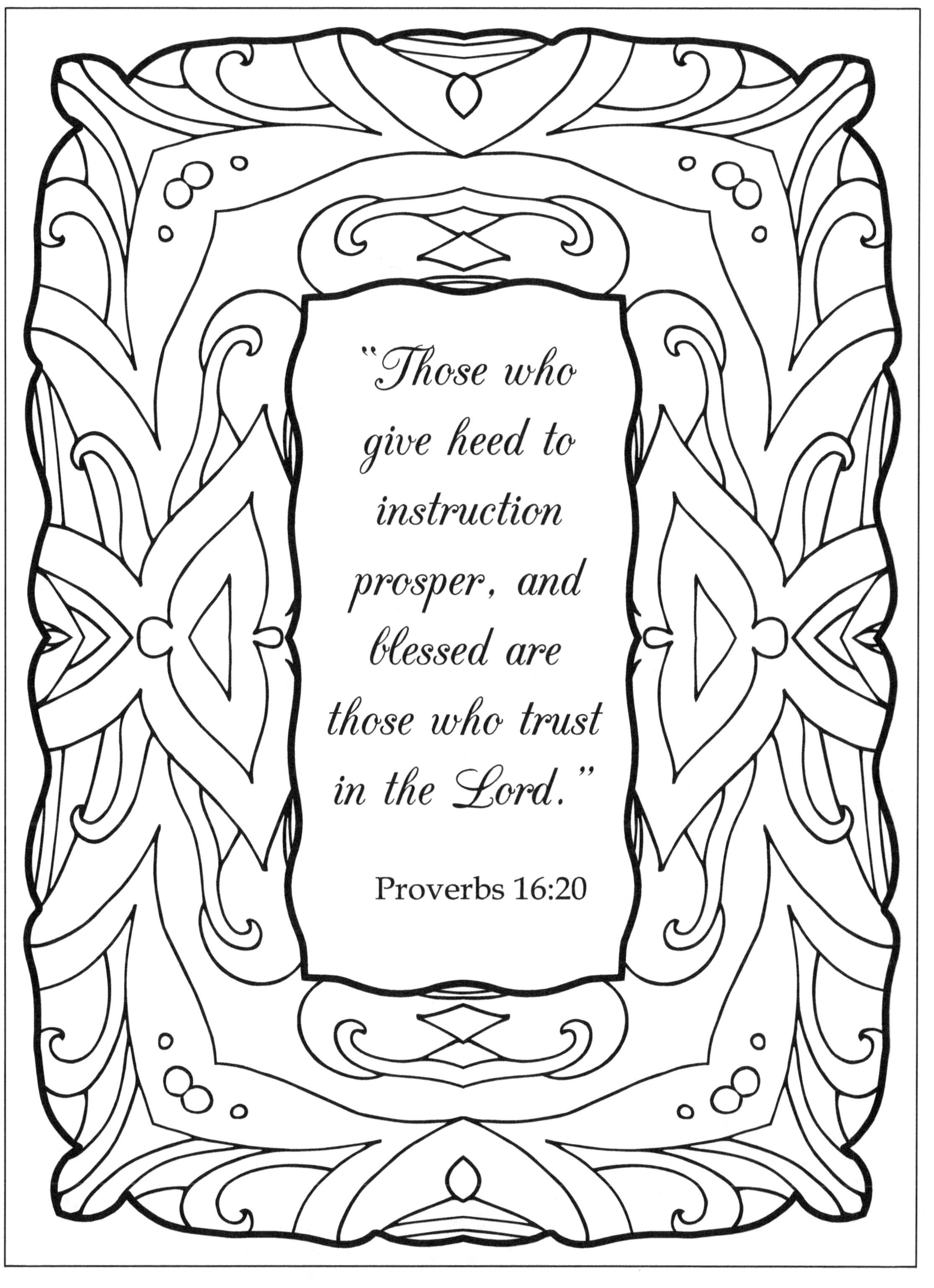
"Those who give heed to instruction prosper, and blessed are those who trust in the Lord."

Proverbs 16:20

"An honest answer is like a kiss on the lips."
Proverbs 24:26

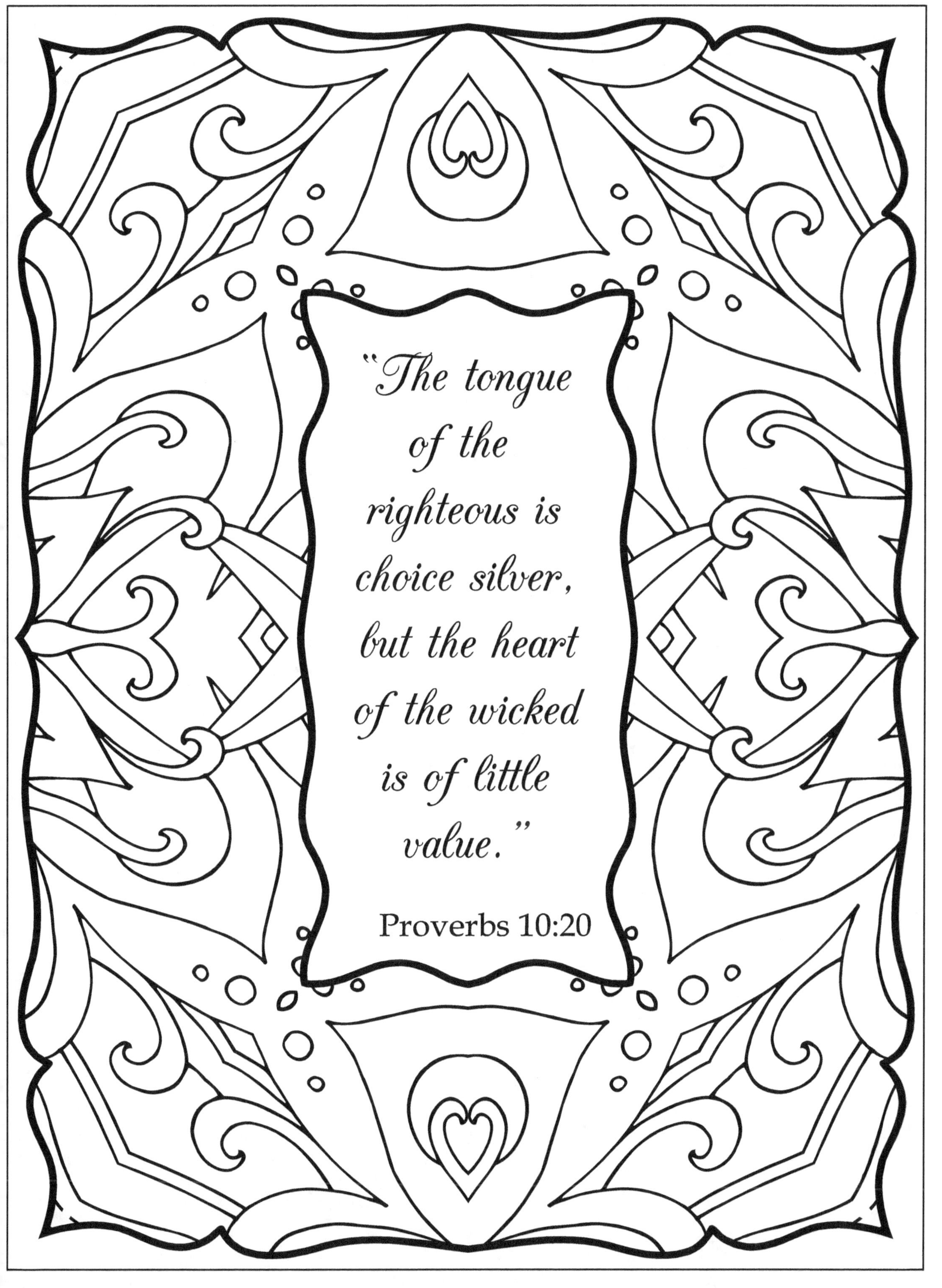
"The tongue
of the
righteous is
choice silver,
but the heart
of the wicked
is of little
value."

Proverbs 10:20

"If you are wise, your wisdom will reward you; if you are a mocker, you alone will suffer."

Proverbs 9:12

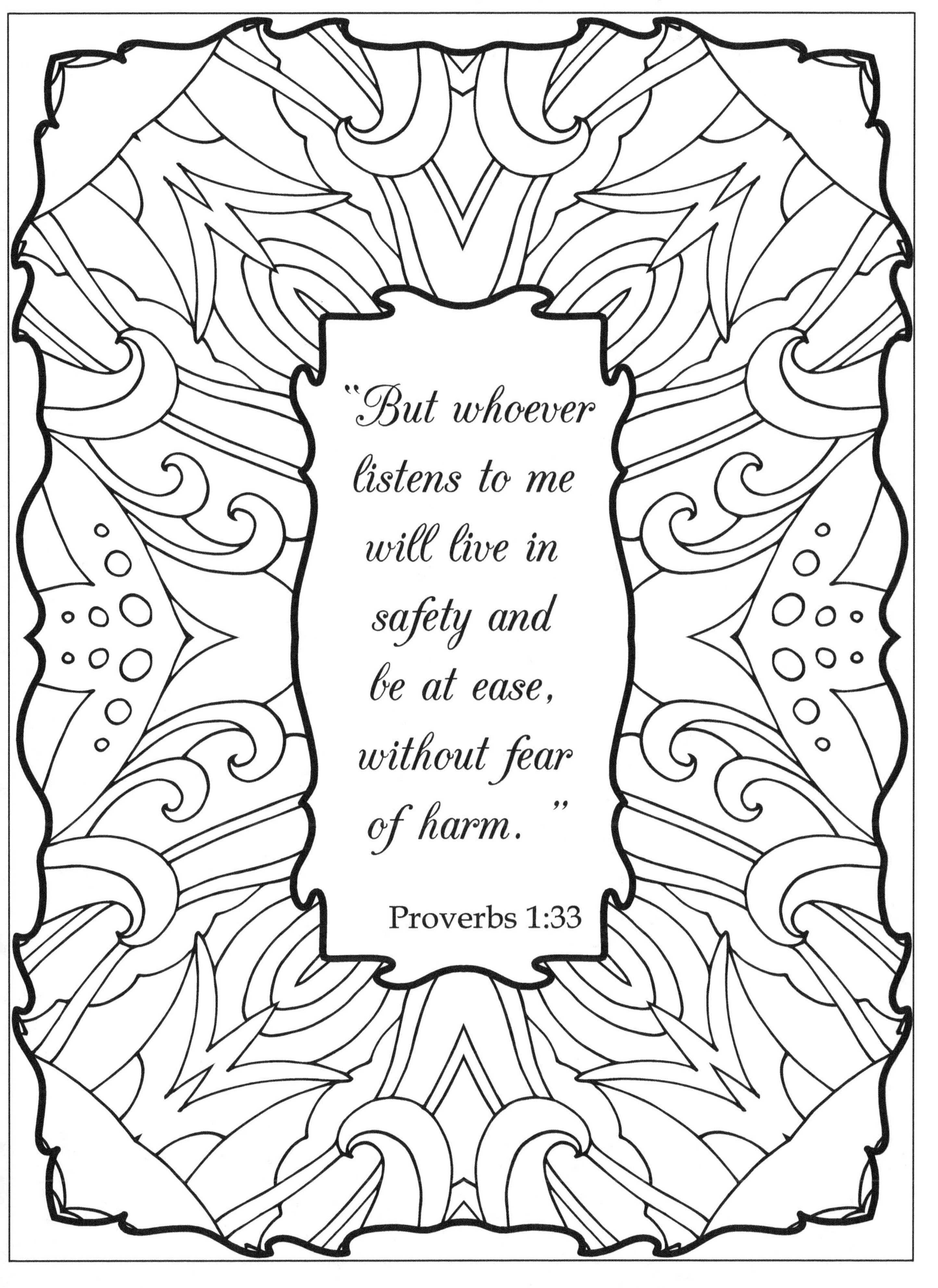

"But whoever listens to me will live in safety and be at ease, without fear of harm."

Proverbs 1:33

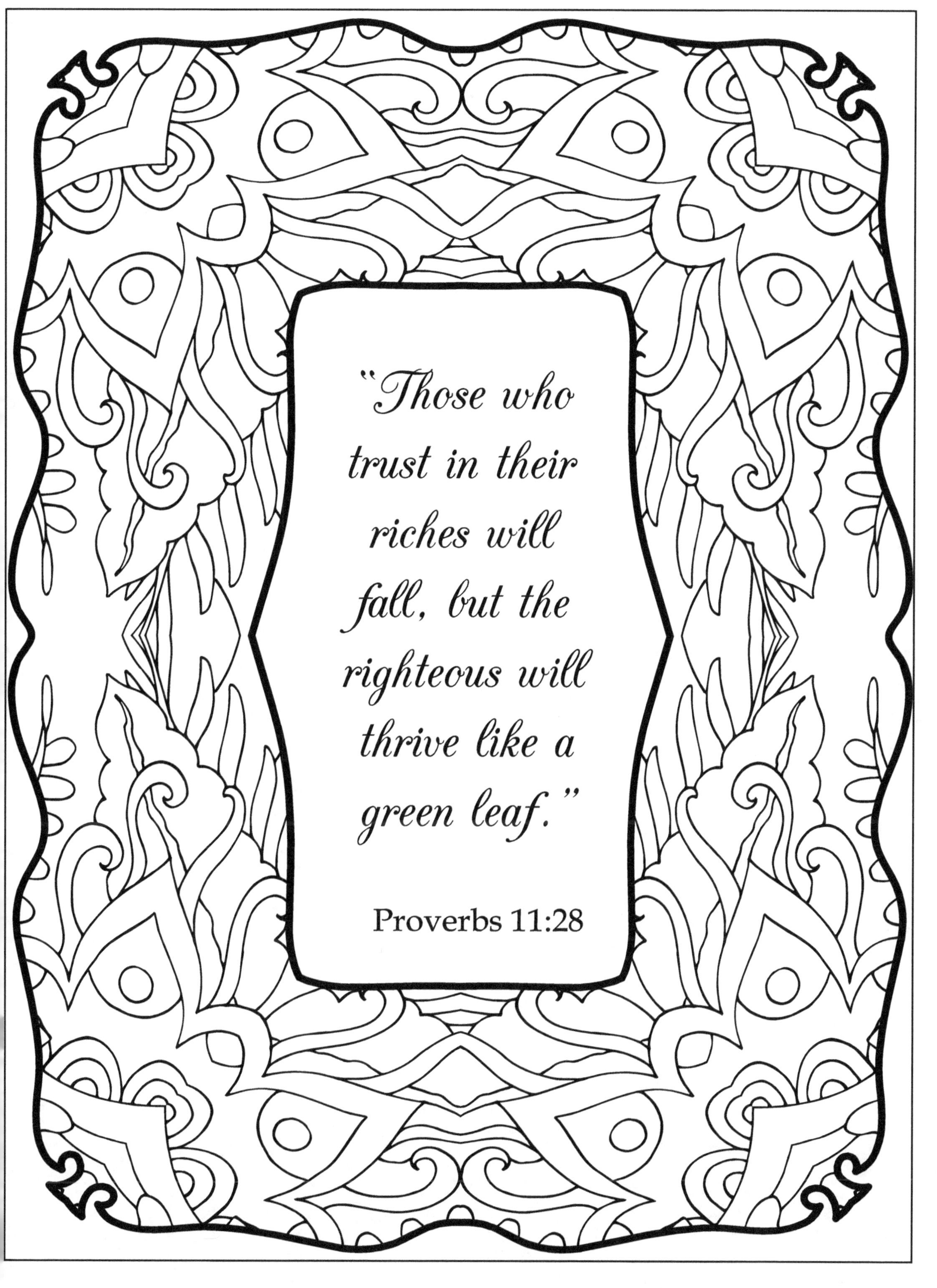

"Those who trust in their riches will fall, but the righteous will thrive like a green leaf."

Proverbs 11:28

"No harm overtakes the righteous, but the wicked have their fill of trouble."

Proverbs 12:21

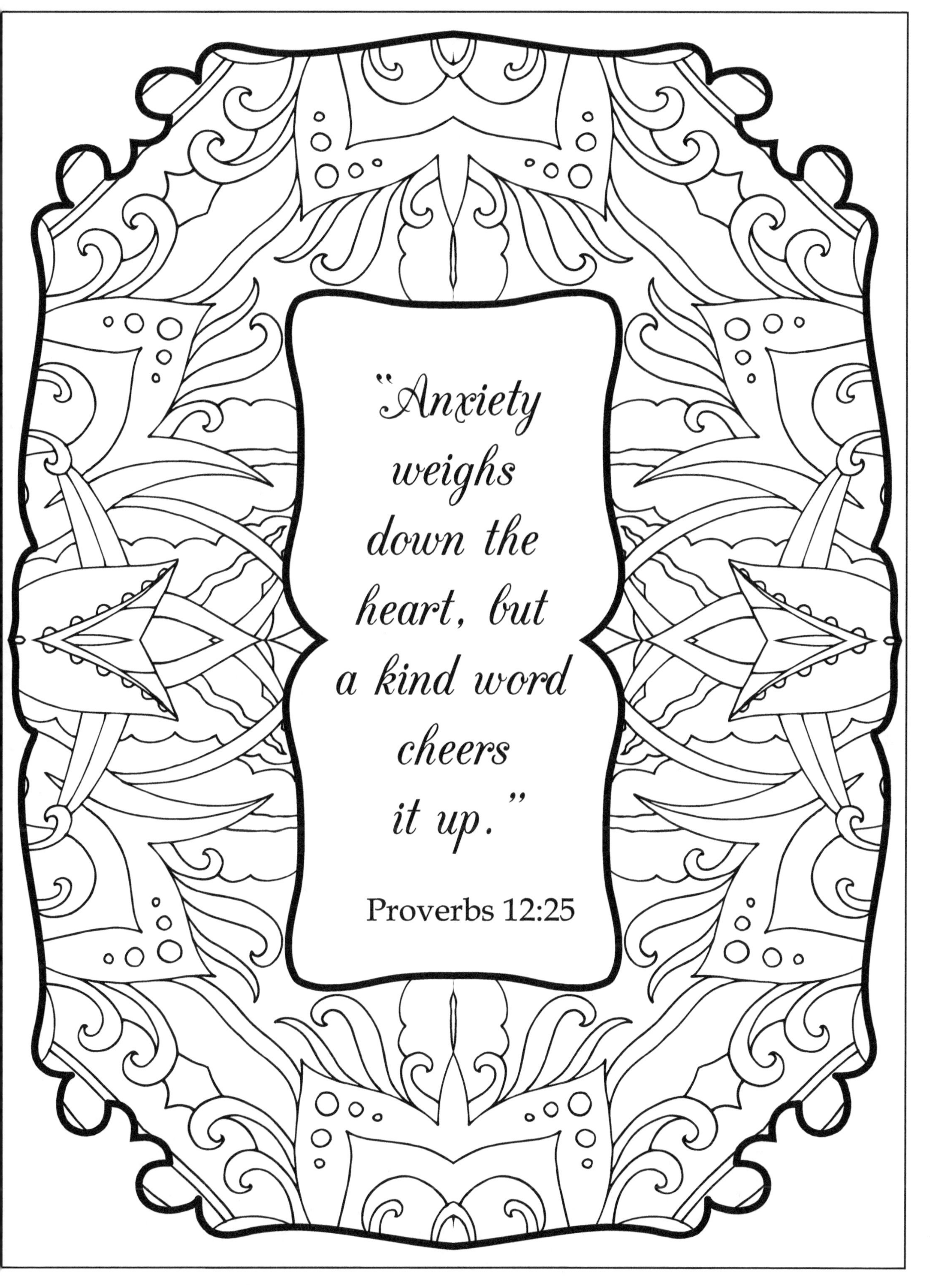

"Anxiety weighs down the heart, but a kind word cheers it up."
Proverbs 12:25

"Her ways are pleasant ways, and all her paths are peace."

Proverbs 3:17

"The fear
of the Lord
leads to life;
then one rests
content,
untouched by
trouble."
Proverbs 19:23

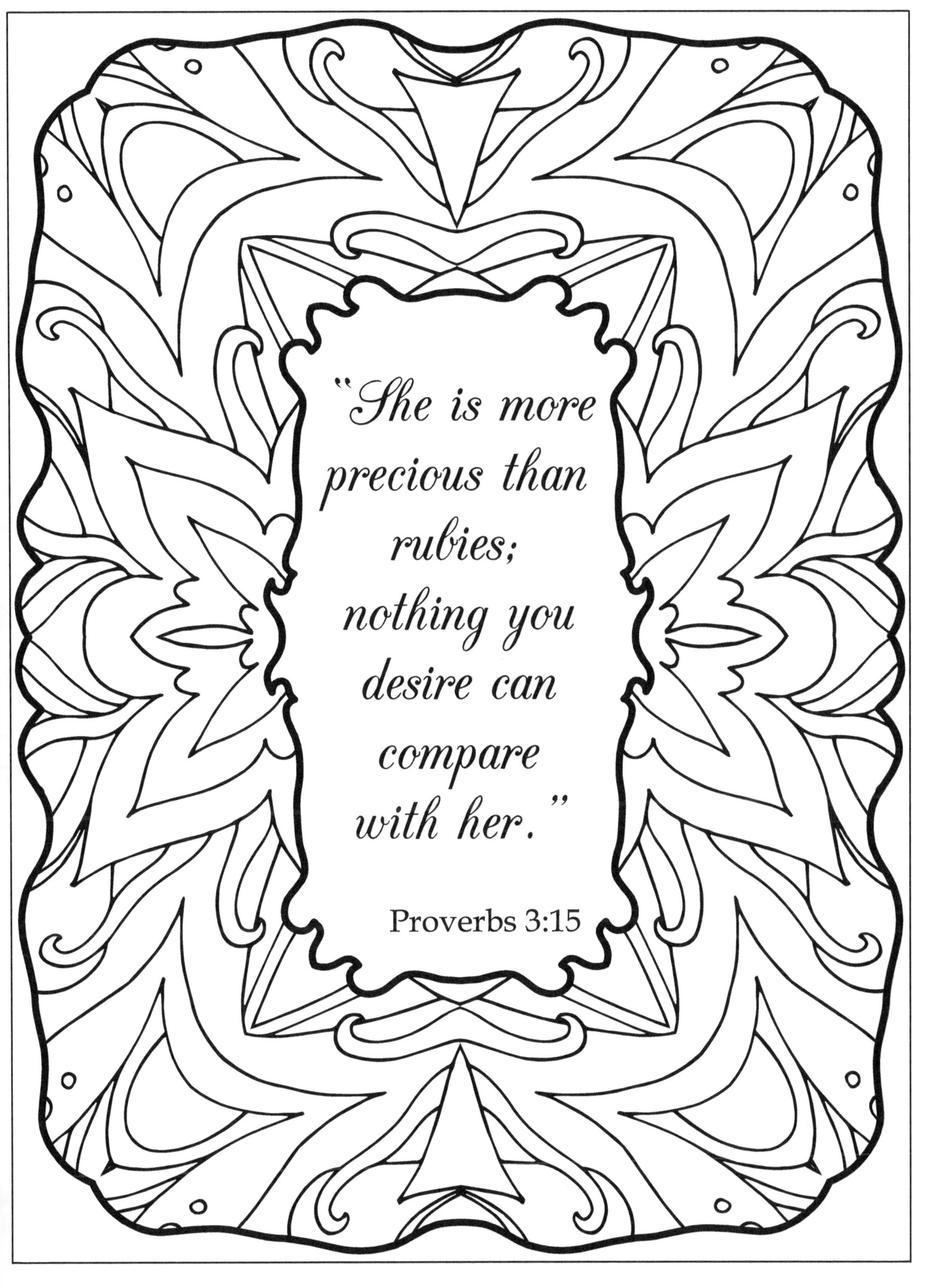
"She is more
precious than
rubies;
nothing you
desire can
compare
with her."

Proverbs 3:15

"A wicked messenger falls into trouble, but a trustworthy envoy brings healing."

Proverbs 13:17

"Whoever seeks good finds favor, but evil comes to those who search for it."
Proverbs 11:27

"Deceit is
in the hearts
of those who
plot evil, but
those who
promote peace
have joy."

Proverbs 12:20

www.ingramcontent.com/pod-product-compliance
Lightning Source LLC
Chambersburg PA
CBHW081152130726
47996CB00009B/3099